"It looks like you have broken your a...," said Mum.
"We will go and see Doctor Lin."

7

"I will look after you,"
said Doctor Lin.
"I will help to fix your arm."

Mo's Broken Arm

written by Anne Giulieri

illustrated by Mark Chambers

"Mum!" said Mo.
"Look at me.
I can go all the way
to the top!"

3

"Oh, yes!" said Mum.
"Can you get to the top?"

Up, up, up went Mo.

"Oh no!" cried Mo.

Down, down, down
went Mo!

"Oh no!" cried Mo.
"My arm is not good!"

"Oh no!" said Mo.
"I cannot go to the top."

Mum and Mo went home.
They sat outside.

"Look!" said Mo.
"A little bird!"

"Oh no!" shouted Mo.

Down, down, down
went the little bird.

"Oh, little bird!" said Mo.
"I will look after you.
I will help you get
to the top."

"Oh, little bird," said Mo.
"Doctor Lin helped me.
I can help you, too!"